Reading Essentials® in Science

ALL ABOUT ANIMALS

Amphibians and Reptiles

JOANNE MATTERN

PERFECTION LEARNING®

Editorial Director:	Susan C. Thies
Editor:	Mary L. Bush
Design Director:	Randy Messer
Book Design:	Tobi Cunningham
Cover Design:	Michael A. Aspengren

A special thanks to the following for his scientific review of the book:
Paul Pistek, Instructor of Biological Sciences,
North Iowa Area Community College

Image Credits:
©Michael & Patricia Fogden/CORBIS: pp. 7 (top), 8 (left), 25; ©Kevin Schafer/CORBIS: p. 8 (right);
©Martin Harvey/CORBIS: p. 14 (bottom); ©David A. Northcott/CORBIS: p. 15;
©Joe McDonald/CORBIS: p. 18 (left); ©Gary Braasch/CORBIS: p. 18 (right);
©Jeffrey L. Rotman/CORBIS: p. 27

Photos.com: front and back cover, all chapter numbers, pp. 1, 3, 4 (bottom), 5 (bottom), 6 (bottom), 9, 10, 12, 14 (top), 17, 19, 20 (top), 20 (bottom), 21 (top), 22 (bottom), 23, 24, 26, 28, 29, 30, 31, 32;
Corel: pp. 5 (top), 7 (bottom), 20 (middle), 21 (bottom)

For information, contact
Perfection Learning® Corporation
1000 North Second Avenue, P.O. Box 500
Logan, Iowa 51546-0500.
Phone: 1-800-831-4190
Fax: 1-800-543-2745
perfectionlearning.com

1 2 3 4 5 6 PP 10 09 08 07 06 05

Paperback ISBN 0-7891-6611-9
Reinforced Library Binding ISBN 0-7569-4635-2

Table of Contents

Introducing Amphibians and Reptiles

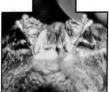    

Amphibians and **reptiles** are some of the most unusual animals in the world. These two animal groups share several characteristics. They also differ from each other in a variety of ways. Let's meet this interesting bunch of creatures!

Alike and Different

Amphibians and reptiles are both **vertebrates**. That means they have a backbone.

Both amphibians and reptiles are **cold-blooded**. Their body temperatures change with the air temperature. When it's hot, they warm up. When it's cold, they cool down.

Most adult amphibians and reptiles have similar ways of moving. They crawl on their bellies or walk on very short legs. Frogs and toads, however, hop on legs that can actually be quite long when stretched out.

Amphibians are creatures of both water and land. These animals are born in water. They stay in the water while they're young. Over time, their bodies change. After these changes, adult amphibians live on land.

Some reptiles live near or in water, but many do not. Reptiles can even live in the desert where it's very dry.

Some amphibians and reptiles are large and frightening. The open jaws of an angry alligator could scare anyone! Other amphibians and reptiles are quiet and shy. Many lizards, for example, are so good at hiding that you can walk past without noticing them.

All in the Family

More than 4500 species of amphibians live on Earth today. These species are divided into several major groups. They include salamanders, newts, frogs, toads, and caecilians.

A Note About Newts

Newts are actually members of the salamander family.

There are many types of reptiles too. Snakes, turtles, tortoises, lizards, alligators, crocodiles, and tuataras are members of the reptile family. More than 6500 different species of reptiles roam the planet today.

Prehistoric Reptiles

The dinosaurs that lived millions of years ago were reptiles.

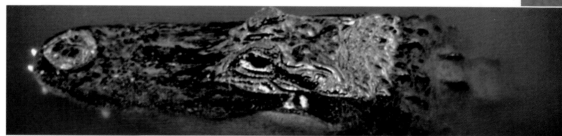

Alligator

2 **Body** Basics

Amphibians and reptiles come in all shapes and sizes. Here are the facts about these creatures and their bodies.

Presto, Chango! I'm an Amphibian!

Most animals have the same bodies all of their lives. Their bodies get bigger or longer, but they keep the same shape and form. Amphibians do things differently! These creatures have two bodies—one for their life in the water and another for their life on land. The change in their bodies is called *metamorphosis*.

More Than One Life

The word *amphibian* comes from the Greek word *amphibious. Amphi* means "both." *Bios* means "life." So amphibians lead "both" lives—one in the water and one on land.

Most amphibians lay their eggs in the water. When the eggs hatch, the young swim away. At this stage, the tiny young animals are called *larvae*. Larvae have **gills** for breathing underwater. They also have bodies made for swimming.

Frogs and toads are a great example of how amphibians go through metamorphosis. When most frogs and toads hatch, they're called *tadpoles*. Tadpoles have gills and round, fat bodies. They don't have legs, but they have a tail that propels them through the water.

As tadpoles grow, their bodies change. Their tails are replaced by four legs. Their eyes become bigger and rounder. Their mouths get bigger too. Lungs grow inside their bodies, and the gills disappear. Now the tadpole is called a *froglet* or *toadlet*. Soon it is able to leave the water and live on land. When it has completed its metamorphosis, the adult animal is called a *frog* or a *toad*.

Red-eyed leaf frog tadpole

Inside Changes

Some types of salamanders go through metamorphosis before they hatch. Their eggs have large yolks that feed the babies as they grow and change. When the salamanders are born, they have adult bodies.

Toad

Scientists divide amphibians into three groups. One group has tails. This group includes salamanders and newts. The second group does not have tails. This group includes frogs and toads. Caecilians make up the third group. Caecilians have no arms or legs. They look like worms.

Caecilian

Except for the caecilians, all amphibians have four legs. The front legs have four toes on each foot. The back feet have five toes each.

Amphibians have to stay wet or their bodies will dry out. They have a special thin skin to help them stay moist. Special glands in the skin produce slime that keeps the amphibians wet.

Reptile Style

Reptiles are divided into four groups. The first group includes snakes and lizards. The second group is made up of crocodiles and alligators. The third group is turtles and tortoises. The fourth group has just one member—the tuatara.

One of a Kind

The tuatara lives in just one place—New Zealand. This reptile is the only surviving member of a family of reptiles that lived at the same time as the dinosaurs. Tuataras have soft, scaly skin and spikes running along their backs. They live in burrows and hunt at night.

Some reptiles are very large. Crocodiles and alligators can be more than 16 feet long and weigh several hundred pounds. Other reptiles are small. Some lizards are just a few inches long and weigh only a few ounces.

Reptile bodies vary. Lizards, crocodiles, alligators, and tuataras have long tails and four legs. Snakes have no legs at all! Turtles and tortoises have hard shells on their backs.

All reptiles have cool, dry skin. Their outer skin is made of scales. These scales provide a tough, protective covering for the animals.

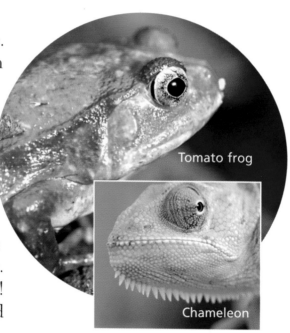

Tomato frog

Chameleon

More in Common Than You Thought

If you thought you had nothing in common with reptiles, think again. The scales on a reptile are made of keratin. This is the same material found in your fingernails, hair, and the top layer of your skin.

That Makes Sense!

Most amphibians and reptiles have good eyesight. A frog's bulgy eyes can see forward, backward, above, and to both sides. This helps frogs sense even the smallest movement. Chameleons can move each eye on its own. This means the lizard can look in two different directions at the same time.

Most amphibians and reptiles don't have ears that can be seen on the outside of their bodies. These animals do, however, have inner organs that help them hear. Iguanas and frogs have thin eardrums in the skin behind their eyes. Snakes and salamanders "hear" animals by sensing vibrations in the air and on the ground.

The sense of smell is very important in the animal world. Amphibians have two sense organs for smell. One is inside the mouth, and the other is at the tip of their nose. Snakes and lizards have a special organ above their mouth that picks up smells and tastes from the air.

The skin is the largest sense organ on an amphibian's or reptile's body. Both types of animals respond to touch and will move quickly if something bothers them.

A Sixth Sense

Snakes and lizards can also sense heat. This helps them know when **warm-blooded prey** are close enough to catch and eat.

Cycles of Life 3

How does an amphibian or reptile grow up? Let's take a look at these animals' lives from birth to death.

In the Beginning

Almost all amphibians and reptiles begin life inside an egg. Female amphibians lay thousands of eggs at once, normally in water. The eggs usually look like blobs of jelly.

Most amphibians don't take care of their young. They just lay eggs and leave. Some salamanders, however, do guard their eggs until they hatch.

Frog Egg Facts

- Some frogs lay 20,000 eggs at one time!
- Several species of frogs have special parts in their bodies where eggs develop before they're laid. These "brood chambers" can be on the neck or back of the frog.

Most reptiles lay eggs too. But unlike amphibians, they lay their eggs on land. A reptile's eggs have a thick, tough shell. The female reptile usually lays her eggs in a safe, damp place. A hole in the ground or under a rock is a good place. Loggerhead turtles dig holes in the sand to lay their eggs.

Crocodile

When reptiles hatch, they look just like their parents, only a lot smaller. Most reptiles don't take care of their young either. Mother crocodiles, however, *do* take care of their babies. They even carry them around in their mouths!

Growing Up Is Hard to Do

The world is a very dangerous place for young amphibians and reptiles. Fish gobble up amphibian eggs. Mammals and birds eat reptile eggs. Baby amphibians and reptiles are prey for fish, birds, and mammals too. For example, sea birds will attack baby turtles as they make their way to the ocean. Out of thousands of eggs, only a small number will actually hatch and develop into adults.

Because they are left on their own, amphibians and reptiles are born knowing how to take care of themselves. Their main job is to eat so they grow bigger and stronger. It doesn't take long before they are adults and can defend themselves.

Staying Safe

Amphibians and reptiles are skilled at protecting themselves from **predators**. One of the best ways to stay safe is to hide. Frogs, salamanders, newts, and small snakes and lizards stay out of sight by hiding under rocks or leaves. The caecilian digs underground **burrows**.

Camouflage helps many amphibians and reptiles stay safe. The color of these animals helps them blend in with their surroundings. A brown lizard lying on brown sand is very hard to see. So is a green frog sitting on a green leaf. A lizard called a *chameleon* can even change its color to camouflage itself in different surroundings.

Inquire and Investigate: Protective Coloring

Question: How does protective coloring help an animal?

Answer the question: I think that protective coloring helps an animal _____.

Form a hypothesis: Protective coloring helps an animal _____.

Test the hypothesis:

Materials
- 30 toothpicks of assorted colors (including green, brown, and blue)
- string
- watch or stopwatch

Procedure
- Record how many of each color toothpick you have.
- Find an area of grass. Use the string to box off a square area about 10 feet by 10 feet.
- Ask someone to drop the toothpicks randomly around the square. Don't watch while he or she does this!
- See how many toothpicks you can find in 30 seconds. Record the number and color of the toothpicks you found. Notice which colors were left. Were certain colors harder to find?

Observations: The green toothpicks should be harder to find. Brown ones or dark blue ones may also be harder to find depending on the color of the grass.

Conclusions: Protective coloring helps an animal by making it blend into its environment. This keeps predators from finding it. Just like the green toothpicks, a green lizard would be harder to spot in the grass than a bright orange one.

Some amphibians and reptiles have clever ways of protecting themselves. Turtles and tortoises have hard shells. If these animals feel scared, they'll draw their legs and heads inside their shells to stay safe.

Snapping turtle

T Is for . . .

What's the difference between a turtle and a tortoise? Turtles live in or around water. Tortoises live on land.

Several types of lizards can puff up their bodies to appear big and scary. This also makes the lizards look too big to eat.

If a predator grabs the tail of certain kinds of lizards, the tail will break off. The lizard can then escape. Later it will grow a new tail.

Many snakes and lizards can bite their enemies. Only a few of these bites are poisonous. Rattlesnakes, copperheads, water moccasins, and coral snakes have poisonous bites. The Gila monster and Mexican beaded lizard are the only two lizards that inject their enemies with venom, or poison. The Komodo dragon has a dangerous bite because deadly bacteria live in its mouth and are spread when the lizard bites something.

Komodo dragons

A variety of amphibians protect themselves by secreting harmful or poisonous substances onto their skin. The substance makes them taste bad and can make predators sick or even kill them. Poison dart frogs are at least polite about their poison. The bright coloring of these frogs warns others to stay away.

Some reptiles are so big and scary, they don't have to worry too much about predators. The Komodo dragon and the Nile monitor lizard are big, fierce predators. So are crocodiles, alligators, and large snakes such as rattlesnakes, pythons, and cobras.

Python

Life as an Adult

Adult amphibians and reptiles spend most of their time looking for food and trying to control their body temperatures. These animals spend much of the day moving from one place to another in search of the right temperature. Large rocks are good places to soak up the sun. Underground burrows, the shade under a rock, or a cool lake or stream are good places to cool off.

Reptiles that live in the desert are usually **nocturnal**. They sleep during the hot day. When the sun goes down, they come out to hunt for food.

In colder parts of the world, amphibians and reptiles can't stay active during the winter. Instead, they find a safe place to **hibernate**. Large groups of snakes will curl up together in a cave or inside a log. Frogs and turtles will find shelter in the mud by a pond or river. Lizards and salamanders curl up under rocks or leaves. During the winter, hibernating amphibians and reptiles live off the fat stored in their bodies. In the spring, they wake up and become active again.

15

4 What's for Dinner?

Amphibians and reptiles eat a variety of foods. From large animals to insects to plants, different amphibians and reptiles have very different diets.

Give Me Meat!

Most amphibians and reptiles are **carnivores**, or meat eaters. Crocodiles and alligators are big meat eaters. They eat a variety of other animals, from birds and fish to antelope and sharks. Frogs and toads eat snails, spiders, worms, crayfish, and baby birds.

Large lizards catch and eat small birds, mice, and other mammals. Some big lizards are fierce predators. The Komodo dragon can kill and eat pigs and goats.

Salamanders will eat almost any other small animal, including fish. They will even eat other salamanders!

Insects are a big part of many reptile and amphibian diets. Frogs and toads feast on insects such as crickets and flies. Caecilians enjoy earthworms, termites, and other insects.

Swallowing with Your Eyeballs?

To swallow their food, frogs close their eyes to press their eyeballs down. The eyeballs push the food into the frogs' stomachs.

Parsons chameleon

Lizards also eat insects. Chameleons have tongues that are as long as their bodies (about 6 inches long). They flick out their sticky tongues to grab passing insects. Other lizards chase insects and grab them with their mouths.

Eggs are a favorite food of many reptiles. Crocodiles, alligators, and snakes steal eggs out of nests and eat them. Because eggs are full of food for growing babies, they are very nutritious for predators.

A Big Gulp

Snakes have teeth, but they cannot chew. Instead, they swallow their prey whole. A snake can even swallow an animal that is bigger than itself.

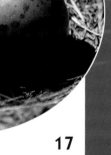

I Prefer Plants

Some amphibians and reptiles only eat plants. These animals are **herbivores**. Many tortoises are herbivores. Tortoises don't move fast enough to catch other animals. Instead, they eat plants and fruits. A few iguanas and **skinks** also eat nothing but plants.

A Spiky Snack

The Galapagos land iguana eats cactus plants. This animal has a special stomach that digests the plant and passes the sharp spines out of its body.

A Bit of Both Please

Amphibians and reptiles that eat both meat and plants are **omnivores**. Many turtles are omnivores. They eat insects and small animals such as snails, frogs, and crayfish. They also feed on plants such as sea grass and lily pads.

A few lizards are omnivores. The beaded lizard eats crickets and worms as well as lettuce and other plants. Basilisks enjoy a diet of small animals, insects, and flowers.

Skink

Basilisk

Hanging Out 5

Where can you find amphibians and reptiles? Swimming in a pond, hiding in the woods, scurrying across the desert, sunning in your backyard garden—almost anyplace can be home to these creatures.

A House for an Amphibian

Almost all amphibians live in or near water. Ponds, lakes, swamps, rivers, and streams are perfect homes for frogs, toads, salamanders, and newts. Besides offering food and moisture, these places provide shelter and protection. Amphibians can hide under rocks or plants in the water or along the shore.

Amphibians also live in woods and forests. Salamanders and frogs, for example, often live under damp leaves and rocks on the forest floor.

Newt

Some amphibians, such as toads, live in grasslands and deserts. Desert amphibians spend most of their time staying cool under rocks or in underground burrows.

Caecilians spend most of their lives in burrows. They live in warm, wet places in Central America, South America, Asia, and Africa.

You might even have amphibians living in your backyard! Cities and suburbs are home to many frogs, toads, and salamanders. These animals live in gardens and parks. They can even be found along wet drainage ditches near busy highways.

Home Sweet Reptile Home

Reptiles can also make their home in many different places. Alligators, crocodiles, and turtles spend most of their lives in the water. Swamps, lakes, ponds, oceans, and drainage ditches provide homes for many of these creatures.

Leopard frogs can live almost anywhere land and water meet.

Spotted salamanders prefer hardwood forests with ponds.

Alligators hang out in freshwater swamps and marshes.

Many reptiles live in the desert. Rattlesnakes, tortoises, and some lizards are desert animals. Like amphibians, these animals spend much of the day staying out of the hot sun. They come out in the cool evenings to find food.

Snakes, turtles, and lizards can also be found in forests. Some live in cool **deciduous** or evergreen forests. Others prefer hot tropical rain forests.

It's Too Cold

The only places amphibians and reptiles can't live are the very cold areas in the extreme northern and southern parts of the planet. Their cold-blooded bodies can't survive the freezing temperatures.

Sidewinder rattlesnake

6 What's Up with Amphibians and Reptiles?

Amphibians and reptiles are found around the globe. Yet these creatures face many threats to their survival. Over the past 25 years, world populations of both amphibians and reptiles have fallen at alarming rates. What is causing this drop and what can be done to stop it?

Rock frog

22

Technology Link

An organization called Conservation International is working to save amphibians and reptiles. The organization's Center for Applied Biodiversity Science is involved in several protection programs for these species. One of these is the Global Amphibian Assessment (GAA).

The GAA's goal is to increase knowledge of the amphibians on Earth. Scientists hope to collect information on every amphibian species on the planet. When the program started, fewer than 1000 species had been written about. Today the GAA has data for almost 5500 species.

Technology allows this information to be shared around the world. The data is available on the Internet through **http://amphibiaweb.org**. This site helps scientists share facts, determine where amphibians are disappearing, and identify threats to these animals. The site also helps scientists examine how changes in **habitats** affect the animals that live there. Hopefully the GAA's work will help decrease the number of disappearing amphibians and reptiles.

Where Did My Home Go?

The biggest danger to amphibians and reptiles is the loss of habitat. People cut down forests. They build houses on the prairie or in the desert. They fill in swamps and other wetlands. All of these actions destroy animal homes.

When their homes are destroyed, amphibians and reptiles have nowhere to live. They also may lose their food supply. No home and no food means no survival for these animals.

Keep It Clean!

Pollution is another danger to amphibians and reptiles. Oil spills, pesticides, and toxic waste poison the water and land. Acid rain pollutes lakes, ponds, and other bodies of water. These harmful substances can make amphibians and reptiles sick or even kill them. The thin skin of amphibians makes it especially easy for poisons to enter their bodies.

Pollution doesn't just affect adult animals. Water pollution destroys amphibian eggs. Air pollution has caused a hole in the Earth's ozone layer. This layer protects the planet from harmful ultraviolet (UV) rays from the Sun. Stronger UV rays can damage amphibian and reptile eggs and affect body formation. This means that new generations of amphibians and reptiles won't even be born or may be born with **deformities**.

A few varieties of frogs complete their metamorphosis within their eggs. They are released as froglet hatchlings instead of tadpoles.

Scientist of Significance

Dr. Stanley Sessions is a biologist who studies frog deformities. In the 1980s, Dr. Sessions began noticing large numbers of frogs with leg deformities. Some frogs had only one back leg. Others had four, six, or even ten back legs!

What was causing the change in the number of frog legs? At first, Dr. Sessions and his students thought that pollution was damaging the frogs' bodies. However, Dr. Sessions soon discovered that pollution was not the reason. The real reason was a tiny worm called a *trematode*.

Trematodes are tiny organisms that burrow into tadpoles' skin and form small sacs called *cysts*. When Dr. Sessions studied deformed frogs, he discovered many trematode cysts around their back legs. The trematodes were getting in the way when the legs developed. This meant that the frogs' legs were blocked or split into two or more legs as they formed.

Dr. Sessions and many other scientists believe that the number of trematodes has increased. That's why there are so many deformed frogs. Scientists continue to investigate the increase in the trematode population. Some believe it may be caused by pollution, which makes it easier for trematodes to grow.

Dr. Sessions and his frogs show just how important balance is in nature. A change in one organism's population can greatly affect another species.

Help Is on the Way

There are many current efforts to protect amphibians and reptiles. Governments and private organizations work to save habitats and reduce pollution. Some endangered species, such as the Puerto Rican crested toad, are now being bred in zoos to increase their populations.

Amphibians and reptiles have inhabited the Earth for more than 325 million years. It's up to everyone to make sure they continue to live on the planet for millions of years to come.

Several species of green turtles are either threatened or endangered due to overhunting by humans and the loss of nesting sites.

Internet Connections and Related Reading for Amphibians and Reptiles

http://animal.discovery.com/guides/atoz/atoz.html
Explore the Animal Planet. Use the "amphibians" or "snakes and reptiles" links to find out more about these amazing animals.

http://nationalzoo.si.edu/Animals/ReptilesAmphibians/ForKids/default.cfm
Visit the Smithsonian National Zoological Park's "Reptiles and Amphibians for Kids" site. Read fun facts, print out pictures to color, and complete amphibian and reptile jigsaw puzzles.

http://www.EnchantedLearning.com/coloring/
Click on "amphibians" or "reptiles" for information and printout sheets on a variety of these interesting creatures.

http://www.pittsburghzoo.com/wildlife_lookUPAnimal.asp
Check out several different amphibians and reptiles at the Pittsburgh Zoo's Web site.

* * * * * * * *

Tree frog

Amazing Crocodiles and Reptiles by Mary Ling. Text and photographs describe amazing members of the world's most remarkable reptiles. Knopf Books, 1991. [RL 4 IL 1–5] (4264401 PB)

Amphibians by Melissa Stewart. This book describes the basic behavior, physical traits, and life cycles of amphibians. Children's Press, 2001. [RL 3 IL 3–5] (6888101 PB 6888106 HB)

Classifying Amphibians by Louise and Richard Spilsbury. Explains what amphibians are and how they differ from other animals, offering an overview of the life cycle of several types of amphibians. Heinemann Library, 2003. [RL 3 IL 3–5] (3453701 PB)

Classifying Reptiles by Louise and Richard Spilsbury. Explains what amphibians are and how they differ from other animals, offering an overview of the life cycle of a variety of reptiles, including snakes, turtles, lizards, and crocodiles. Heinemann Library, 2003. [RL 3 IL 3–5] (3454201 PB)

Reptiles by Melissa Stewart. This book describes the basic behavior and physical traits of reptiles. Children's Press, 2001. [RL 3 IL 3–5] (6885501 PB 6885506 HB)

•RL = Reading Level
•IL = Interest Level
Perfection Learning's catalog numbers are included for your ordering convenience. PB indicates paperback. HB indicates hardback.

Emerald tree boa

Glossary

amphibian (am FIB ee en) cold-blooded animal that reproduces in water but lives its adult life on land (see separate entry for *cold-blooded*)

burrow (BER oh) hole or tunnel dug by an animal for a home

camouflage (KAM uh flahzh) protective coloring or other characteristics that help an animal blend in to its environment

carnivore (KAR nuh vor) animal that eats mostly meat

cold-blooded (kohld BLUHD ed) having a body temperature that depends on air temperature

deciduous (di SID jyou uhs) having trees that lose their leaves in the fall

deformity (di FOR muh tee) change from normal body structure

gill (gil) organ on fish and other animals used to breathe underwater

habitat (HAB i tat) place where a plant or animal lives

herbivore (ER buh vor) animal that eats mostly plants

hibernate (HEYE ber nayt) to go into a sleeplike state during the winter

Green iguana

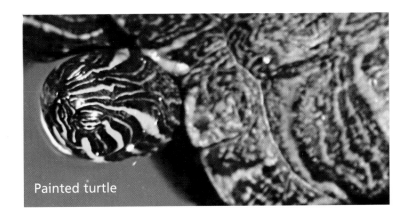
Painted turtle

nocturnal (nahk TERN uhl) active at night rather than during the day

omnivore (AHM nuh vor) animal that eats both meat and plants

predator (PRED uh ter) animal that hunts other animals for food

prey (pray) animal that is hunted by other animals for food

reptile (REP teyel) air-breathing animal with scales

skink (skingk) small, smooth lizard with a long, thin body and small limbs

vertebrate (VER tuh brayt) animal with a spine or backbone

warm-blooded (warm BLUHD ed) having a body temperature that doesn't depend on air temperature

Land iguana

Index

Tomato frog